Financial Success Made Easy

Getting What You Want

by

Frank Figliomeni

Financial Success Made Easy   Frank Figliomeni
Getting What You Want

Financial Success Made Easy Frank Figliomeni
Getting What You Want

All Rights Reserved. No part of this publication may be reproduced in any form or by any means, including scanning, photocopying, or otherwise without prior written permission of the copyright holder being Frank Figliomeni.

Copyright © 2017

Table of Contents

Introduction 7

What is Money 9

Why you need Money. 10

When to Start Building Wealth. 12

Lay the Proper Mental Foundation. 16

    Get a Positive Attitude. 16

    Use Time Effectively. 18

    Upgrade your skills and network. 19

Start with the End in Mind 20

How to Make Money. 21

    Get a Job 22

    Be your own Boss 24

    Sole ownership 26

    Proprietorship 28

- Corporation or Incorporation 30
- Positive Cash Flow. 31
  - What is an Asset. 32
  - What is a Liability... 35
  - Get Other Source of Income. 38
  - Time and Money 39
  - Ways to Increase Your Wealth. 42
    - Savings.. 43
    - Stocks.. 44
    - Mutual Funds 45
    - Real-estate.. 47
- Insurance 49
- Debt Reduction 50
- Taxes Deductions, Refunds and Coupons 52
- Wills... 54
- Your Personal Plan. 55

Create a Budget...64

Tracking Expenses (Workbook) 66

Financial Plan 97

Financial Plan Goals Worksheet......................................98

Conclusion..99

Introduction

This book is dedicated to all those people who are striving for the goal of being in good shape financially.

This book will provide some understanding on how to increase your finances which may lead to being rich. The key word is 'may' as this is not a scam to give you delusions of following a few simple tricks and suddenly you will be rich. If you want a quick and easy guide to being rich I need to let you know it does not exist. Wealth is built with some fundamental steps that can increase the odds of being rich.

If you think reading this book will suddenly make you rich without any work on your part then think again. If all you are willing to do is drink beer and watch TV or stay on the computer watching videos this is not for you.

You will need to do work and at times it can be difficult yet if you persevere you can reap a better financial future.

Let us start this journey to get you going on your ways to a better life.

What is Money

I am going to give a brief overview of how money came into being. This is what all people in society need in order to exchange goods or services.

In the past there was no money, people used the barter system. The Barter system is basically exchanges what one person had for something someone else had. An example would be I give you three chickens for a baby goat. As time passed this became more impractical so slowly the barter system was replaces by coins - silver or gold. These metals have value of themselves and still do so today.

As time progressed paper money was introduced which was backed by gold of that country. This gave the paper money value since it was backed by gold. In the 1970's in USA the gold backing was moved to oil backing the dollar. Currently in some countries the paper money is only guaranteed by that government.

Why you need Money.

The reason we need money is to survive. You need money to pay for shelter, food, clothing - the basics of life. You need money to pay the bills. There are some people who will say that money is not everything and that is true yet if you do not have any money you better get used to living on the street. Without money you cannot take care of the basics of life or the luxuries of life such as taking a vacation.

Since you are reading this book I take you understand what I just stated as if you didn't have any money you could not have purchased this book.

One reason you purchased this book was to learn how to increase your wealth - you want more money to enjoy the better things in life.

With more money you can go from using the bus to owning your own car or if you have a car to getting a better one.

You can get a better house, wardrobe, take vacations and other material possessions.

If you have money you can support local charities or help those around you, that is your choice.

The main point is it is better to have more money that to have less than you need or none at all.

When to Start Building Wealth.

The best time to start build your wealth is when you are young. The younger the better. In today's society the young people have little understanding of wealth building and are more concerned with enjoyment. Many young boys and some girls will spend money that they do have on self indulgence. For example, video games, video consoles, toys, parting and other items.

If you were to tell them to save money or to invest money they have received whether through gifts, part time jobs etc. they will look at you strange.

The Western Society is consumer based and it encourages the citizens to spend money on entertainment, personal products etc. This keeps the economy growing as more money spent means jobs are required which makes it good for business.

There is nothing wrong with spending some money for yourself - you do not want to be a miser wearing one set of clothes. You must start looking at a means to use some of the money you have to increase your wealth.

The sooner you start the better due to compound interest and time. To increase wealth you must learn compound interest and use it to your advantage.

all money used properly can make you incredible rich.

Even a penny if you double it daily in 30 days would make you a millionaire.

Here is the sample.

Day 1: $.01
Day 2: $.02
Day 3: $.04
Day 4: $.08
Day 5: $.16
Day 6: $.32
Day 7: $.64
Day 8: $1.28
Day 9: $2.56
Day 10: $5.12
Day 11: $10.24
Day 12: $20.48
Day 13: $40.96
Day 14: $81.92
Day 15: $163.84
Day 16: $327.68
Day 17: $655.36
Day 18: $1,310.72
Day 19: $2,621.44
Day 20: $5,242.88
Day 21: $10,485.76
Day 22: $20,971.52
Day 23: $41,943.04
Day 24: $83,886.08
Day 25: $167,772.16
Day 26: $335,544.32

Day 27: $671,088.64
Day 28: $1,342,177.28
Day 29: $2,684,354.56
Day 30: $5,368,709.12

In thirty days you are a millionaire just by doubling a penny. You need to learn to use all available money to work for you and create more money.

Lay the Proper Mental Foundation.

In order to be successful in finance you will need to have a certain mindset. I have listed those which I believe are the main ones to get what you want.

Get a Positive Attitude.

in order to get what you want you have to believe you will achieve your goal. Being positive will carry you during the times when things get rough in your endure for success.

Most people stop going for their goals because they lack a positive attitude. When things get off track on the road to achieving the goal the let fear take over and then stop going for the goal.

I can't express how much having a positive attitude is necessary to achieve the goal in anything in life. Many rich people failed time and time again yet they had a positive attitude and persevered until finally they reached the goal.

Always remember if it was easy then everyone would be rich.

Most people take the easy road in life and lead a simple, poor or middle class life. If you want to make it big you have to be able to handle the rough times and rejection. This is why you need a positive attitude to succeed.

Use Time Effectively.

Plan your daily activities in order to maximize your chances to achieve your goal. This means to stop or at least reduce watching television and other social media unless it brings you closer to your goal. Stop wasting time on daily time wasters such as people who waste your time on gossip and meaningless nonsense.

Get yourself a small blank notepad and track how you spend your day. You will see how you spend your day and I am certain you will be amazed how much time you waste.

You are precious and so is your time. Stop wasting your time!

Upgrade your skills and network.

In this day it is easy to be replaced in a job. If you have a company and you are doing the same thing over and over then others will soon pass you by. You need to be away of what is new and how it may affect you in either your job or business.

You also should join groups which deal in the same field you are interested in to achieve your goal. If you want to be rich then join groups which deal with the subject of wealth.

Get yourself a mentor who is already successful and learn all you can from that person.

Start with the End in Mind

Everyone is different and the values will vary person from person. You must start your journey to wealth creation with the end in mind. You must set for yourself a goal that you want to obtain and determine when you want that goal to be reached.

How much wealth do you want to have that will make you happy and comfortable. Do you want to have a house paid off, money in the bank that is a million dollars with stocks?

Our society is based in instant self gratification and many people will spend money on frivolous items to provide a momentary gratification. In order to build wealth then you must have a plan in place and start working in order to obtain your final goal.

Do not keep your plan as an idea rather put it on paper and remind yourself daily of what your goal is and start putting your plan into action.

How to Make Money.

In order to build wealth you need to have some money in order for it to grow. Unless you are born a prince/princess or have inherited millions then you like most of us need to start making money prior to increasing your wealth.

The first method which you should NOT do is to engage in illegal activities such as selling drugs, armed robber etc.

Do not do these activities.

Now to the law abiding ways to make and build wealth.

Get a Job

The most common method to start making money is you need to get some type of job. When you are in high school try getting a part-time job in order to make some money.

For those who are in school or out of school the following applies to get a job.

Get a resume setup and check for spelling. Send it to all the companies in your area and go in person if you can as some companies prefer to see you in person as they receive multitudes of resumes and it is easy to be just another name on a list.

You need to stand out and going in person makes you stand out. For more professional positions you cannot go in person yet if you can contact the hiring manager via phone or email that is a plus on your side.

Make sure for the interview that you are well dressed and clean to improve your chances of getting that position. If you are dressed looking like a slob then you will definitely decrease your chance of getting that position.

Before you go to the interview be prepared by learning what the company does and know about the position you applied.

During the interviewer use a firm hand shake. You should present yourself as confident and make the interviewer know ways ***you can help the company***.

Remember it is not about you rather it is about how you can help the company that will get you the job. At the end either you will be offered job on the spot or if not, ask what the next steps are such as when he/she will determine who will be hired.

Send a follow up email thanking the interviewer for the time spent and again restate your interest in the position. This is to make you stand out and give you a greater chance to get that position.

Be your own Boss

The problem with getting a job is that it limits you to a certain amount of money you can make. You get either an hourly rate or a salary for your time. In order to increase your wealth then you may need to look at getting another job or being your own boss.

There are some drawbacks to a job such as the illusion that you have a steady pay cheque. Notice I said illusion as you can be terminated from your position at anytime. The company can decide to downsize and suddenly you have no position.

You may be or know someone who went to work and gets called into the bosses office and human resources is present. They are given their walking papers. This is hard to grasp yet a job is not forever. Most people fall into that illusion and live their life as if they will always be working at their position. If you decide to stay at a job just understand that you are limiting yourself to a specific income which can end suddenly.

If you want to give yourself the option of unlimited income then you will need to move to another way of thinking and working.

The higher the risk you are willing to take the greater the return. Before you venture to start a business you should assess if you have what it takes as some people are content to just work at a job - 9 to 5 and get a steady pay cheque.

One way to give yourself the chance for higher income is to be your own boss either full-time or a more cautious method via a part-time business.

There are several types of businesses you can start. I will give you a brief overview of each.

Sole ownership

You own the company and make all the decisions being the sole owner. This type of business gives you a greater personal freedom to grow your business.

Pro:

The pros to this is that you are the only owner and do not have to deal with another person to make decisions.

You get to chose when to work and how long you want to work.

You do not have to ask to take time off .

Cons:

A major con is that you are responsible if anything happens 'personally'. If you do a job which has issues you can be sued and they can go after your personal assets. Many people do not go this route as you can lose your life savings if something happens which you are held accountable.

If you do not chose to work you will not make any many. This can impact your business as customers may need you and since you are unavailable will go elsewhere.

Health benefits are covered by yourself which can be high in cost.

If you are seriously ill you have no income to cover you and you can end up losing your business and/or your house.

Proprietorship

This is when two or more people own one business. This is a step above the sole proprietor.

Pro:

The pro is that you have someone helping grow the business and greater chance to grow the business.

If you are off the business can still run as the partner can step in.

You can bounce ideas of someone else and avoid some business mistakes.

Con:

The con is you need to both agree for a decision to be made regarding business direction.

One partner may have a different direction for the company which can lead to arguments and stressful situations.

You are legally responsible for your partners conduct. If the partner does something that is illegal or damaging (business related) then you are also accountable and can be sued. For example your partner takes all the business cash and leaves the country. You are held accountable to meet your client responsibilities and can be sued if you do not plus you just lost all that money.

Many people decide against this due to the exposure you have to being sued and losing everything.

Corporation or Incorporation

Most people decide to start a company as this insulates the owner from personal legal liabilities.

Pro:

The pro is that you and the company are two separate entities. If someone sues the company for any reason then they can go against the company yet not after your own personally assets.

In the event the company goes bankrupt for whatever reason then you are not affected as you are a separate entity.

A company name is more professional and appealing to clients. People have more confidence in a corporation instead of some guy someone told you about who does some work. Someone your friend knows.

Cons:

The cons is the additional cost to incorporate. You need to spend money to get yourself incorporated.

Positive Cash Flow.

We have gone over some ways to generate money yet now is time to deal with how to keep the money and grow wealth.

In order to move forward you must understand assets, liabilities, other sources of income to create a positive cash flow.

What is an Asset.

An asset can be defined as a useful or desirable quality.

In general accounting terms a car is considered an asset as is a house. A computer is an asset a television is an asset.

We are conditioned to obtain assets by the media, our parents and society in general. Does having assets make you rich? Well, not necessarily.

When I tell people this they look at me strange. They will say I have a house and can sell it and make more money than what I paid for it.

The people who lost their houses during the recession in 2008 would disagree. When you sell your house you need someone to buy it for more than you paid that is true yet if the market falls you may have no buyers. The cost for mortgage and taxes etc. make it easier to sell and lose than keep drowning in debt.

The other issue is to maintain a house which depending on the cost making it cheaper to rent.

Neither of these options is beneficial to create wealth. In regards to wealth creation I would define an asset is an investment or any item which generates an income giving a positive cash flow.

Should you decide to purchase a house you need to look at renting part of the house. The renter who pays you will offset your costs.

Here is an example:

<u>Monthly Cost</u>

Mortgage	$ 1,200.00
Land Tax	$ 300.00
Utilities	$ 300.00
Total Cost	**$ 1,800.00**

<u>Monthly Income</u>

Renter 1	$ 950.00
Renter 2	$ 950.00
Total Income	$1,900.00

<u>Positive Income $ 100.00 monthly</u>

In this example you are living free and making $100.00 every month. Based on your personal cost and rental costs in your area this will change yet you get the idea.

You need a renter to cover your costs if possible or at least reduce your costs which gives you more free money in order to invest.

What is a Liability.

A liability is a good or service you must pay for and in accounting and example would be accounts payable.

Many people are conditioned very young to get a good education and then a get a good paying job with growth potential. After this then society says buy a new car and take vacations. The only problem with this situation is although it may feed your ego and make you happy at first, there is still the matter of the debt you now have to pay off. . By putting yourself in debt you will now have a difficult time getting out of that debt and little chance of creating wealth. You need to get out of personal debt in order to create wealth.

Debt that is to create wealth is different and I will address that later.

Personal debt is a great enemy and must be overcome. You need to check your purchases and not be overly self indulgent in your spending.

If you spend on items which may create wealth then this is good - such as an education. The money you spend to educate yourself will increase potential for wealth creation yet you need to get rid of that loan ASAP.

Personal debt (bad debt) for example, a new car is a major liability. A car is an expense and not an asset. You need to pay a monthly fee to pay off the loan or pay for the rental of the car. You need to pay the car insurance and then the gas to get you around in the car. Then you must pay for general maintenance and car repairs when it breaks down. Notice how much money is being spent to own and maintain the car.

If you really need a car I suggest you get yourself a solid used car and let someone else lose the 30% on the new car purchase. I believe a car depreciates 30% once driven off the lot - maybe more or less.

When you want to sell the car you never get your money back. A car is a luxury and guaranteed to lose you money.

Now let us look at home ownership. This can be a liability or an asset. You do need to live somewhere so some money will go out from your pocket. A house needs you to cover the mortgage payments, taxes, utilities and then general repairs or any upgrades.

Renting may be a better option yet renting is making someone else rich. Renting or owning a home and living by yourself is a liability. Yet owning a home and renting can be an asset.

If you buy a home then you can make it an asset by having part of it rented.

Get Other Source of Income.

You should look at ways to create other sources of income. Other sources of income can be writing a book, music –teaching or creating songs, create a blog. There are other sources you can look into yet it is helpful to have other sources of income.

In order to be wealthy you need more than one source of income to reach that goal. It may be time consuming and hard to do as you will be tired after doing a full day's work.

Regardless of being hard you should look into this as it has the potential of making you very wealthy if it succeeds. The other reason is that if you lose your main income – 'the job' you have other sources of income and losing a job will be less stressful as you are not dependant on that one source of income.

Time and Money

One of the main concepts you need to understand and put into practice it that have separating your time from a money. What I mean by this is that to start you need to leverage time for money via a job and then possible a business or you are fortunate directly to a business.

Even in a business your time is money and you have only a certain amount of time in a day.

Let us say you are making $100.00 an hour. What would you have at the end of the year?

Hourly rate $ 100.00

8 hours $800.00

5 Days a week $ 4,000.00

52 weeks $ 208,000.00

Now remember you still have to pay taxes so let us remove 30% for taxes.

You are now left with $ 145,600.00.

That is a really good pay yet how many people make $100.00 an hour? Maybe some lawyers and doctors but that is not the wage of the average person.

You want to position yourself that your money is not tied into your time. Ever wonder why musicians are so rich?

The reason is that their time is not tied to the hourly rate. When a musician makes a hit song he/she receives royalties based on the number sold. They also receive income for airplay on radio stations. While they are sleeping people all over the world are either buying or listening on the radio to their song and the musician gets money. What a life to do something once and get paid even when you are sleeping.

Let us take for example large store - I will not use a specific company. When people go the store and purchase products or services the owner is making money. You will notice that the wealth is not tied to the owners time doing work rather on the item or service being sold.

Let us take for example YouTube where people of successful channels are paid royalties for the amount of views(ads) when there video is monetized.

To really get to great wealth you want to eventually aim for this goal.

Do not trade time for money.

Ways to Increase Your Wealth.

When you get your pay cheque or if you chose to be a business owner how do you use the money?

In order to create wealth then do not do what most do which is to spend everything being self indulgent. They live pay cheque to pay cheque. I understand you may want to get that new video game or new clothes, cologne or perfume and by all means do so as you only live once. My point is that you need to take a portion of what you make and put that away and do not touch that money.

You can do the 10% rule which states the whatever you make you put the 10% aside in saving or some type of investment. If you can put more away then I suggest you do so to speed up the wealth increase.

Savings

You can put the 10% from your earning into a savings account yet with interest rates so low you will see little growth in the investment.

The benefit is that for the most part the money is secure yet you may lose some money on monthly fees. You should get a savings account with no monthly fee - this depends on your banks policy.

Stocks

You can invest in stocks and preferably ones that provide a dividend. This means that you get a certain amount of money per share per period. Should the stock increase your money has also increased yet the issue is that the stock can go down and you can lose money. You need to also take into account there is also the cost for purchasing the stock or selling it pending which options is chosen.

Stock can make you really rich or can make you lose everything on a downturn. Be careful if e\investing in stocks. Get as much information on the company and seek professional help on this one.

Mutual Funds

This method will allow more flexibility of choices. There are funds which are more for the conservative person which provide a guaranteed amount or at least will secure the original amount invested.

There are other funds which are more for the higher risk taker which provide a potential greater return yet have a chance for a greater lose if the fund tanks. These funds are more volatile. For mutual funds you need to discuss with a representative to determine your level of comfort. My suggestions is that if you are young and at the start of a job/business then go for a more volatile fund. If you do lose then you have time to recover the money back.

If you are middle aged then I suggest a mix of volatile and conservation funds. You need to protect you income to a point yet you would need some funds to take a chance for greater return.

If you are looking at retiring or retired you should be heavily in conservative funds and guaranteed funds. At this point in your life you need to protect what you have earned as you do not have time to make up the money if it goes down.

Real-estate

This is a very tricky one to deal with. In order to get into real-estate you need money for a down payment and also need to get a mortgage of some type. This debt is good in the sense that the goal is to use the debt to create greater wealth. Buying a piece of land and selling it a few years later at a greater cost can increase your wealth. The risk is that if the land value goes down and this can happen. In this case you lose money if you need to sell so just be aware of this fact.

<u>Do not fall for the scam that you always make money on real-estate.</u>

Some people purchase a house to rent to others. They may live in part of it or rent the whole house. If you can get rental income that covers the mortgage and taxes and have the renter handle the utilities you make a positive cash flow. In time the house cost should usually go up yet it can decline - just be aware.

The other issue you need to deal with is problem renters which do not pay or damage your property. You may be stuck trying to get them out while they live at your house for free. Do you have enough money to cover the cost of a mortgage if they don't pay and legal fees?

You should do a background check on the potential renters yet this may reduce the chance of getting a 'professional renter'.

Professional renters will rent houses or apartments and soon after will not pay the rent. They know the law and use it to live rent free for a period of time until they find another place to rent and do the same thing all over again. They will cost you plenty to get rid of so be aware.

Should you however end up renting to a good tenant then you can cover the costs and make money which is your goal. Be aware of both sides to this endeavor.

Insurance

Insurance is important to secure your investments and life. If you are married you should have life insurance to protect your loved ones in case of your death. This is not a pleasant thing to address yet there is a reality - no one lives forever. You need to insure that your loved ones would be taken care of if you die - ex. car accident.

The amount of coverage depends on your situation in life - are you just married, one child or several children.

In this case you should discuss this with a life insurance agent to see what fits your current situation and how much coverage you need and can afford.

Debt Reduction

You need to get a handle on your debts. If you went to school and have a student loan then you should be aiming to eliminate that debt ASAP. The benefit of education should provide a higher paying position yet the debt with the interest you are paying is impacting the time it will take to create your wealth.

If you purchased a vehicle or some furniture on credit then you should be targeting to eliminate this debt by putting extra money on your payment to remove this debt.

You want to use interest in order grow your wealth and not having to pay extra interest for any item which makes someone else rich. By paying interest on an item you reduce your wealth and some rates for ex. furniture - the interest can be up to 18%. This may vary pending the financial market. Credit card payments are up to 20% which is a bit hit to your financial plan. It is easy to get seduced by using your credit card for impulse items. That new pair of shoes you just have to have or that new video game etc.

This purchase may give you immediate satisfaction yet you need to prioritize - do you need that item?

Taxes Deductions, Refunds and Coupons

In order to increase your wealth you should take advantage of tax deductions. When you are completing your taxes get all the deductions you can get for yourself. In Canada you can use RRSP's to reduce your taxes and possibly get a refund. In other countries there will be similar tax deductions you can use.

I suggest you get a professional accountant to have them review your taxes and provide you professional advice in order to reduce your taxes.

Another area you should use is coupons which can reduce your cost on regular daily items. Stores usually provide coupons and there are sites which provide a list of coupons and sales.

Check your weekly store flyer in order to take advantage of the sales on grocery or other personal items.

This is an excellent method to cut your costs on a regular bases. Try to avoid paying full price on items as most items at one point may go on sale. I have heard of cases in which people have saved thousands of dollars a year by using coupons. This is time consuming yet the savings may be worth the effort you put in.

Wills

You should have a will drawn up by a lawyer to ensure that your assets are distributed to those you want in case of your death. I suggest you do not do this yourself and get it done by a lawyer who will provide guidance based on your current situation in life.

Your will should be reviewed ever several years or if they is a major change in your life circumstance. I know this will cost extra yet this will avoid much anguish to those left behind having to deal with your death as creating your own will may have items omitted or other issues to numerous to mention.

Your Personal Plan.

Many people read a book and then soon forget what they learned and go back to their old habits. The first step to financial success is to complete this section.

Answer the following question and keep as a reminder to reinforce and remind you daily of your commitment to succeed.

Why do I want to be Wealthy?

Write down the reasons you want to be wealthy to remind you daily and keep you on track.

1)

2)

3)

4)

5)

What am I doing to meet this goal of being wealthy?

1)

2)

3)

4)

5)

6)

What are the benefits of me being wealthy?

1)

2)

3)

4)

5)

6)

What personal or tangible assets do I have to reach my goal?

1)

2)

3)

4)

5)

What may be interfering with my goal?

1)

2)

3)

4)

5)

6)

How will I overcome these obstacles?

1)

2)

3)

4)

5)

6)

What are my goals and milestones dates to measure my progress?

1)

2)

3)

4)

5)

6)

What have I done to correct any problems that have arisen to get me back on track

1)

2)

3)

4)

5)

6)

Create a Budget.

The most common mistake people do is not to create a budget. In order to be financially fit you must know where all your money is going to whether mortgage payments, car payments, bills, personal expenses, luxury items, impulse buying etc.

Get yourself a small book to keep track of all the money you spend and review after a week. You will be shocked to see how much is spent on frivolous items yet adding up to a lot at the end of the week.

If you have a computer or tablet you can get a template or make one to keep track of your spending and investments. You will need to constantly review your spending habits, investments and personal goals or they will get out of control.

Investments need to be checked as there may be a better one yielding better returns. To be financially successful you need to be on top of things and not let other people take control of your finances.

To help you out I added some pages at the end of this book so you can write in your daily expenses.

Remember your financial future is in your hands.

Tracking Expenses (Workbook)

Date _____

I spent money on the following:

Item	My Reason	Cost
_____	_____	____
_____	_____	____
_____	_____	____
_____	_____	____
_____	_____	____
_____	_____	____
_____	_____	____
_____	_____	____
_____	_____	____
_____	_____	____

Financial Success Made Easy Frank Figliomeni
Getting What You Want

Date _____

I spent money on the following:

Item	My Reason	Cost
_____	_____	____
_____	_____	____
_____	_____	____
_____	_____	____
_____	_____	____
_____	_____	____
_____	_____	____
_____	_____	____
_____	_____	____
_____	_____	____

Date _____

I spent money on the following:

Item	My Reason	Cost
_____	_____	___
_____	_____	___
_____	_____	___
_____	_____	___
_____	_____	___
_____	_____	___
_____	_____	___
_____	_____	___
_____	_____	___
_____	_____	___

Financial Success Made Easy   Frank Figliomeni
Getting What You Want

Date _____

I spent money on the following:

Item	My Reason	Cost
_____	_____	____
_____	_____	____
_____	_____	____
_____	_____	____
_____	_____	____
_____	_____	____
_____	_____	____
_____	_____	____
_____	_____	____
_____	_____	____

Date _____

I spent money on the following:

Item	My Reason	Cost
_____	_____	____
_____	_____	____
_____	_____	____
_____	_____	____
_____	_____	____
_____	_____	____
_____	_____	____
_____	_____	____
_____	_____	____
_____	_____	____

Financial Success Made Easy   Frank Figliomeni
Getting What You Want

Date _____

I spent money on the following:

Item	My Reason	Cost
_____	_____	____
_____	_____	____
_____	_____	____
_____	_____	____
_____	_____	____
_____	_____	____
_____	_____	____
_____	_____	____
_____	_____	____
_____	_____	____

Date _____

I spent money on the following:

Item	My Reason	Cost
_____	_____	____
_____	_____	____
_____	_____	____
_____	_____	____
_____	_____	____
_____	_____	____
_____	_____	____
_____	_____	____
_____	_____	____
_____	_____	____

Financial Success Made Easy　　　　　　Frank Figliomeni
Getting What You Want

Date _____

I spent money on the following:

Item	My Reason	Cost
____	_____	___
____	_____	___
____	_____	___
____	_____	___
____	_____	___
____	_____	___
____	_____	___
____	_____	___
____	_____	___
____	_____	___

Date _____

I spent money on the following:

Item	My Reason	Cost
_____	_____	____
_____	_____	____
_____	_____	____
_____	_____	____
_____	_____	____
_____	_____	____
_____	_____	____
_____	_____	____
_____	_____	____
_____	_____	____

Financial Success Made Easy   Frank Figliomeni
Getting What You Want

Date _____

I spent money on the following:

Item	My Reason	Cost
_____	_____	____
_____	_____	____
_____	_____	____
_____	_____	____
_____	_____	____
_____	_____	____
_____	_____	____
_____	_____	____
_____	_____	____
_____	_____	____

Financial Success Made Easy Frank Figliomeni
Getting What You Want

Date _____

I spent money on the following:

Item	My Reason	Cost
_____	_____	___
_____	_____	___
_____	_____	___
_____	_____	___
_____	_____	___
_____	_____	___
_____	_____	___
_____	_____	___
_____	_____	___
_____	_____	___

Financial Success Made Easy — Frank Figliomeni
Getting What You Want

Date _____

I spent money on the following:

Item	My Reason	Cost
_____	_____	____
_____	_____	____
_____	_____	____
_____	_____	____
_____	_____	____
_____	_____	____
_____	_____	____
_____	_____	____
_____	_____	____
_____	_____	____

Financial Success Made Easy   Frank Figliomeni
Getting What You Want

Date _____

I spent money on the following:

Item	My Reason	Cost
_____	_____	___
_____	_____	___
_____	_____	___
_____	_____	___
_____	_____	___
_____	_____	___
_____	_____	___
_____	_____	___
_____	_____	___
_____	_____	___

Financial Success Made Easy — Frank Figliomeni
Getting What You Want

Date _____

I spent money on the following:

Item	My Reason	Cost
_____	_____	____
_____	_____	____
_____	_____	____
_____	_____	____
_____	_____	____
_____	_____	____
_____	_____	____
_____	_____	____
_____	_____	____
_____	_____	____

Financial Success Made Easy Frank Figliomeni
Getting What You Want

Date _____

I spent money on the following:

Item	My Reason	Cost
_____	_____	____
_____	_____	____
_____	_____	____
_____	_____	____
_____	_____	____
_____	_____	____
_____	_____	____
_____	_____	____
_____	_____	____
_____	_____	____

Financial Success Made Easy Frank Figliomeni
Getting What You Want

Date _____

I spent money on the following:

Item	My Reason	Cost
____	_____	___
____	_____	___
____	_____	___
____	_____	___
____	_____	___
____	_____	___
____	_____	___
____	_____	___
____	_____	___
____	_____	___

Date _____

I spent money on the following:

Item	My Reason	Cost
_____	_____	____
_____	_____	____
_____	_____	____
_____	_____	____
_____	_____	____
_____	_____	____
_____	_____	____
_____	_____	____
_____	_____	____
_____	_____	____

Date _____

I spent money on the following:

Item	My Reason	Cost
_____	_____	____
_____	_____	____
_____	_____	____
_____	_____	____
_____	_____	____
_____	_____	____
_____	_____	____
_____	_____	____
_____	_____	____
_____	_____	____

Financial Success Made Easy Frank Figliomeni
Getting What You Want

Date _____

I spent money on the following:

Item	My Reason	Cost
_____	_____	____
_____	_____	____
_____	_____	____
_____	_____	____
_____	_____	____
_____	_____	____
_____	_____	____
_____	_____	____
_____	_____	____
_____	_____	____

Financial Success Made Easy   Frank Figliomeni
Getting What You Want

Date _____

I spent money on the following:

Item	My Reason	Cost
_____	_____	___
_____	_____	___
_____	_____	___
_____	_____	___
_____	_____	___
_____	_____	___
_____	_____	___
_____	_____	___
_____	_____	___
_____	_____	___

Financial Success Made Easy Frank Figliomeni
Getting What You Want

Date _____

I spent money on the following:

Item	My Reason	Cost
_____	_____	____
_____	_____	____
_____	_____	____
_____	_____	____
_____	_____	____
_____	_____	____
_____	_____	____
_____	_____	____
_____	_____	____
_____	_____	____

Date _____

I spent money on the following:

Item	My Reason	Cost
_____	_____	___
_____	_____	___
_____	_____	___
_____	_____	___
_____	_____	___
_____	_____	___
_____	_____	___
_____	_____	___
_____	_____	___
_____	_____	___

Financial Success Made Easy   Frank Figliomeni
Getting What You Want

Date _____

I spent money on the following:

Item	My Reason	Cost
_____	_____	____
_____	_____	____
_____	_____	____
_____	_____	____
_____	_____	____
_____	_____	____
_____	_____	____
_____	_____	____
_____	_____	____
_____	_____	____

Financial Success Made Easy Frank Figliomeni
Getting What You Want

Date _____

I spent money on the following:

Item	My Reason	Cost
_____	_____	____
_____	_____	____
_____	_____	____
_____	_____	____
_____	_____	____
_____	_____	____
_____	_____	____
_____	_____	____
_____	_____	____
_____	_____	____

Date _____

I spent money on the following:

Item	My Reason	Cost
_____	_____	____
_____	_____	____
_____	_____	____
_____	_____	____
_____	_____	____
_____	_____	____
_____	_____	____
_____	_____	____
_____	_____	____
_____	_____	____

Financial Success Made Easy Frank Figliomeni
Getting What You Want

Date _____

I spent money on the following:

Item	My Reason	Cost
_____	_____	____
_____	_____	____
_____	_____	____
_____	_____	____
_____	_____	____
_____	_____	____
_____	_____	____
_____	_____	____
_____	_____	____
_____	_____	____

Date _____

I spent money on the following:

Item	My Reason	Cost
_____	_____	____
_____	_____	____
_____	_____	____
_____	_____	____
_____	_____	____
_____	_____	____
_____	_____	____
_____	_____	____
_____	_____	____
_____	_____	____

Financial Success Made Easy — Frank Figliomeni
Getting What You Want

Date _____

I spent money on the following:

Item	My Reason	Cost
_____	_____	____
_____	_____	____
_____	_____	____
_____	_____	____
_____	_____	____
_____	_____	____
_____	_____	____
_____	_____	____
_____	_____	____
_____	_____	____

Date _____

I spent money on the following:

Item	My Reason	Cost
_____	_____	____
_____	_____	____
_____	_____	____
_____	_____	____
_____	_____	____
_____	_____	____
_____	_____	____
_____	_____	____
_____	_____	____
_____	_____	____

Financial Success Made Easy
Getting What You Want

Frank Figliomeni

Date _____

I spent money on the following:

Item	My Reason	Cost
_____	_____	____
_____	_____	____
_____	_____	____
_____	_____	____
_____	_____	____
_____	_____	____
_____	_____	____
_____	_____	____
_____	_____	____
_____	_____	____

Financial Success Made Easy   Frank Figliomeni
Getting What You Want

Date _____

I spent money on the following:

Item	My Reason	Cost
_____	_____	____
_____	_____	____
_____	_____	____
_____	_____	____
_____	_____	____
_____	_____	____
_____	_____	____
_____	_____	____
_____	_____	____
_____	_____	____

Financial Plan

To keep track of your finances you will need a financial plan. The plan will indicate your income you make and expenses you incur. The plan will need to be setup and maintained on a regular basis.

There are many sites which you go to which will have samples of financial plans you can download for free. If not you can easy put one together quickly with information from sites.

I suggest bank sites to get the information if you are stuck.

Financial Plan Goals Worksheet

Financial Plan Goals Worksheet

Short-Term Goals (Less than 1 year)					
Priority	Goal	Total Cost	Duration	Monthly Cost	Target Date

Intermediate Goals (1-10 years)					
Priority	Goal	Total Cost	Duration	Monthly Cost	Target Date

Long-Term Goals (Over 10 years)					
Priority	Goal	Total Cost	Duration	Monthly Cost	Target Date

Conclusion

I have provided some guidance for you to reduce your debts and create some wealth. You need to take action for this to work and do not be disappointed with any setbacks as this is common.

You need to always stay in control of your finances and your spending habits.

Remember in all things to enjoy your life, enjoy family, friends, a good meal, a fine drink and vacations.

My other books are available on **Amazon** website.

www.ingramcontent.com/pod-product-compliance
Lightning Source LLC
Chambersburg PA
CBHW061442180526
45170CB00004B/1526